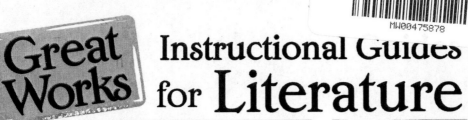

Great Works Instructional Guides for Literature

Number the Stars

A guide for the novel by Lois Lowry
Great Works Author: Suzanne Barchers, Ed.D.

SHELL EDUCATION

Publishing Credits

Kristy Stark, Editor

Image Credits

Shutterstock (cover, p. 12); Image courtesy of Matt McKee (p. 11)

Standards

© 2007 Teachers of English to Speakers of Other Languages, Inc. (TESOL)
© 2007 Board of Regents of the University of Wisconsin System. World-Class Instructional Design and Assessment (WIDA)
© Copyright 2010. National Governors Association Center for Best Practices and Council of Chief State School Officers.
All rights reserved.

Shell Education

5301 Oceanus Drive
Huntington Beach, CA 92649-1030
http://www.shelleducation.com
ISBN 978-1-4258-8985-2
© 2015 Shell Educational Publishing, Inc.

Table of Contents

How to Use This Literature Guide

Today's standards demand rigor and relevance in the reading of complex texts. The units in this series guide teachers in a rich and deep exploration of worthwhile works of literature for classroom study. The most rigorous instruction can also be interesting and engaging!

Many current strategies for effective literacy instruction have been incorporated into these instructional guides for literature. Throughout the units, text-dependent questions are used to determine comprehension of the novel as well as student interpretation of the vocabulary words. The novels chosen for the series are complex exemplars of carefully crafted works of literature. Close reading is used throughout the units to guide students toward revisiting the text and using textual evidence to respond to prompts orally and in writing. Students must analyze the story elements in multiple assignments for each section of the novel. All of these strategies work together to rigorously guide students through their study of literature.

The next few pages will make clear how to use this guide for a purposeful and meaningful literature study. Each section of this guide is set up in the same way to make it easier for you to implement the instruction in your classroom.

Theme Thoughts

The great works of literature used throughout this series have important themes that have been relevant to people for many years. Many of the themes will be discussed during the various sections of this instructional guide. However, it would also benefit students to have independent time to think about the key themes of the novel.

Before students begin reading, have them complete *Pre-Reading Theme Thoughts* (page 13). This graphic organizer will allow students to think about the themes outside the context of the story. They'll have the opportunity to evaluate statements based on important themes and defend their opinions. Be sure to have students keep their papers for comparison to the *Post-Reading Theme Thoughts* (page 64). This graphic organizer is similar to the pre-reading activity. However, this time, students will be answering the questions from the point of view of one of the characters of the novel. They have to think about how the character would feel about each statement and defend their thoughts. To conclude the activity, have students compare what they thought about the themes before they read the novel to what the characters discovered during the story.

How to Use This Literature Guide (cont.)

Vocabulary

Each teacher overview page has definitions and sentences about how key vocabulary words are used in the section. These words should be introduced and discussed with students. There are two student vocabulary activity pages in each section. On the first page, students are asked to define the ten words chosen by the author of this unit. On the second page in most sections, each student will select at least eight words that he or she finds interesting or difficult. For each section, choose one of these pages for your students to complete. With either assignment, you may want to have students get into pairs to discuss the meanings of the words. Allow students to use reference guides to define the words. Monitor students to make sure the definitions they have found are accurate and relate to how the words are used in the text.

On some of the vocabulary student pages, students are asked to answer text-related questions about the vocabulary words. The following question stems will help you create your own vocabulary questions if you'd like to extend the discussion.

- How does this word describe _____'s character?
- In what ways does this word relate to the problem in this story?
- How does this word help you understand the setting?
- In what ways is this word related to the story's solution?
- Describe how this word supports the novel's theme of . . . .
- What visual images does this word bring to your mind?
- For what reasons might the author have chosen to use this particular word?

At times, more work with the words will help students understand their meanings. The following quick vocabulary activities are a good way to further study the words.

- Have students practice their vocabulary and writing skills by creating sentences and/or paragraphs in which multiple vocabulary words are used correctly and with evidence of understanding.

- Students can play vocabulary concentration. Students make a set of cards with the words and a separate set of cards with the definitions. Then, students lay the cards out on the table and play concentration. The goal of the game is to match vocabulary words with their definitions.

- Students can create word journal entries about the words. Students choose words they think are important and then describe why they think each word is important within the novel.

How to Use This Literature Guide (cont.)

Analyzing the Literature

After students have read each section, hold small-group or whole-class discussions. Questions are written at two levels of complexity to allow you to decide which questions best meet the needs of your students. The Level 1 questions are typically less abstract than the Level 2 questions. Level 1 is indicated by a square, while Level 2 is indicated by a triangle. These questions focus on the various story elements, such as character, setting, and plot. Student pages are provided if you want to assign these questions for individual student work before your group discussion. Be sure to add further questions as your students discuss what they've read. For each question, a few key points are provided for your reference as you discuss the novel with students.

Reader Response

In today's classrooms, there are often great readers who are below average writers. So much time and energy is spent in classrooms getting students to read on grade level, that little time is left to focus on writing skills. To help teachers include more writing in their daily literacy instruction, each section of this guide has a literature-based reader response prompt. Each of the three genres of writing is used in the reader responses within this guide: narrative, informative/explanatory, and argument. Students have a choice between two prompts for each reader response. One response requires students to make connections between the reading and their own lives. The other prompt requires students to determine text-to-text connections or connections within the text.

Close Reading the Literature

Within each section, students are asked to closely reread a short section of text. Since some versions of the novels have different page numbers, the selections are described by chapter and location, along with quotations to guide the readers. After each close reading, there are text-dependent questions to be answered by students.

Encourage students to read each question one at a time and then go back to the text and discover the answer. Work with students to ensure that they use the text to determine their answers rather than making unsupported inferences. Once students have answered the questions, discuss what they discovered. Suggested answers are provided in the answer key.

How to Use This Literature Guide (cont.)

Close Reading the Literature (cont.)

The generic, open-ended stems below can be used to write your own text-dependent questions if you would like to give students more practice.

- Give evidence from the text to support . . . .
- Justify your thinking using text evidence about . . . .
- Find evidence to support your conclusions about . . . .
- What text evidence helps the reader understand . . . ?
- Use the novel to tell why _____ happens.
- Based on events in the story, ...
- Use text evidence to describe why . . . .

Making Connections

The activities in this section help students make cross-curricular connections to writing, mathematics, science, social studies, or the fine arts. Each of these types of activities requires higher-order thinking skills from students.

Creating with the Story Elements

It is important to spend time discussing the common story elements in literature. Understanding the characters, setting, and plot can increase students' comprehension and appreciation of the story. If teachers discuss these elements daily, students will more likely internalize the concepts and look for the elements in their independent reading. Another important reason for focusing on the story elements is that students will be better writers if they think about how the stories they read are constructed.

Students are given three options for working with the story elements. They are asked to create something related to the characters, setting, or plot of the novel. Students are given a choice on this activity so that they can decide to complete the activity that most appeals to them. Different multiple intelligences are used so that the activities are diverse and interesting to all students.

How to Use This Literature Guide (cont.)

Culminating Activity

This open-ended, cross-curricular activity requires higher-order thinking and allows for a creative product. Students will enjoy getting the chance to share what they have discovered through reading the novel. Be sure to allow them enough time to complete the activity at school or home.

Comprehension Assessment

The questions in this section are modeled after current standardized tests to help students analyze what they've read and prepare for tests they may see in their classrooms. The questions are dependent on the text and require critical-thinking skills to answer.

Response to Literature

The final post-reading activity is an essay based on the text that also requires further research by students. This is a great way to extend this novel into other curricular areas. A suggested rubric is provided for teacher reference.

Correlation to the Standards

Shell Education is committed to producing educational materials that are research and standards based. As part of this effort, we have correlated all of our products to the academic standards of all 50 states, the District of Columbia, the Department of Defense Dependents Schools, and all Canadian provinces.

Purpose and Intent of Standards

Standards are designed to focus instruction and guide adoption of curricula. Standards are statements that describe the criteria necessary for students to meet specific academic goals. They define the knowledge, skills, and content students should acquire at each level. Standards are also used to develop standardized tests to evaluate students' academic progress. Teachers are required to demonstrate how their lessons meet standards. Standards are used in the development of all of our products, so educators can be assured they meet high academic standards.

How to Find Standards Correlations

To print a customized correlation report of this product for your state, visit our website at http://www.shelleducation.com and follow the online directions. If you require assistance in printing correlation reports, please contact our Customer Service Department at 1-877-777-3450.

Correlation to the Standards (cont.)

Standards Correlation Chart

The lessons in this guide were written to support the Common Core College and Career Readiness Anchor Standards. This chart indicates which sections of this guide address the anchor standards.

Common Core College and Career Readiness Anchor Standard	Section
CCSS.ELA-Literacy.CCRA.R.1—Read closely to determine what the text says explicitly and to make logical inferences from it; cite specific textual evidence when writing or speaking to support conclusions drawn from the text.	Close Reading the Literature Sections 1–5; Analyzing the Literature Sections 1–5; Creating with the Story Elements Sections 1–5
CCSS.ELA-Literacy.CCRA.R.2—Determine central ideas or themes of a text and analyze their development; summarize the key supporting details and ideas.	Analyzing the Literature Sections 1–5; Creating with the Story Elements Sections 1, 3, 5; Making Connections Sections 2, 5
CCSS.ELA-Literacy.CCRA.R.3—Analyze how and why individuals, events, or ideas develop and interact over the course of a text.	Analyzing the Literature Sections 1-5; Close Reading the Literature Sections 1–5; Creating with the Story Elements Sections 1–5
CCSS.ELA-Literacy.CCRA.R.5—Analyze the structure of texts, including how specific sentences, paragraphs, and larger portions of the text (e.g., a section, chapter, scene, or stanza) relate to each other and the whole.	Analyzing the Literature Sections 1–5; Creating with the Story Elements Sections 2, 4
CCSS.ELA-Literacy.CCRA.R.10—Read and comprehend complex literary and informational texts independently and proficiently.	Entire Unit
CCSS.ELA-Literacy.CCRA.W.1—Write arguments to support claims in an analysis of substantive topics or texts using valid reasoning and relevant and sufficient evidence.	Reader Response Sections 1, 3, 5; Creating with the Story Elements Section 1; Post-Reading Response to Literature
CCSS.ELA-Literacy.CCRA.W.2—Write informative/explanatory texts to examine and convey complex ideas and information clearly and accurately through the effective selection, organization, and analysis of content.	Reader Response Sections 2–4; Making Connections Section 2; Post-Reading Response to Literature
CCSS.ELA-Literacy.CCRA.W.3—Write narratives to develop real or imagined experiences or events using effective technique, well-chosen details and well-structured event sequences.	Reader Response Sections 1–2, 4–5; Creating with the Story Elements Section 5; Culminating Activity; Post-Reading Response to Literature
CCSS.ELA-Literacy.CCRA.W.4—Produce clear and coherent writing in which the development, organization, and style are appropriate to task, purpose, and audience.	Creating with the Story Elements Section 1; Reader Response Sections 1–5; Culminating Activity; Post-Reading Response to Literature
CCSS.ELA-Literacy.CCRA.W.6—Use technology, including the Internet, to produce and publish writing and to interact and collaborate with others.	Post-Reading Response to Literature
CCSS.ELA-Literacy.CCRA.W.7—Conduct short as well as more sustained research projects based on focused questions, demonstrating understanding of the subject under investigation.	Post-Reading Response to Literature

Correlation to the Standards (cont.)

Standards Correlation Chart (cont.)

Common Core College and Career Readiness Anchor Standard	Section
CCSS.ELA-Literacy.CCRA.W.9—Draw evidence from literary or informational texts to support analysis, reflection, and research.	Creating with the Story Elements Sections 1, 5; Culminating Activity; Post-Reading Response to Literature
CCSS.ELA-Literacy.CCRA.L.1—Demonstrate command of the conventions of standard English grammar and usage when writing or speaking.	Creating with the Story Elements Sections 1, 5; Reader Response Sections 1–5; Culminating Activity; Post-Reading Response to Literature
CCSS.ELA-Literacy.CCRA.L.2—Demonstrate command of the conventions of standard English capitalization, punctuation, and spelling when writing.	Creating with the Story Elements Sections 1, 5; Reader Response Sections 1–5; Culminating Activity; Post-Reading Response to Literature
CCSS.ELA-Literacy.CCRA.L.4—Determine or clarify the meaning of unknown and multiple-meaning words and phrases by using context clues, analyzing meaningful word parts, and consulting general and specialized reference materials, as appropriate.	Vocabulary Sections 1–5
CCSS.ELA-Literacy.CCRA.L.5—Demonstrate understanding of figurative language, word relationships, and nuances in word meanings.	Vocabulary Sections 1–5
CCSS.ELA-Literacy.CCRA.L.6—Acquire and use accurately a range of general academic and domain-specific words and phrases sufficient for reading, writing, speaking, and listening at the college and career readiness level; demonstrate independence in gathering vocabulary knowledge when encountering an unknown term important to comprehension or expression.	Vocabulary Sections 1–5

TESOL and WIDA Standards

The lessons in this book promote English language development for English language learners. The following TESOL and WIDA English Language Development Standards are addressed through the activities in this book:

- **Standard 1:** English language learners communicate for social and instructional purposes within the school setting.

- **Standard 2:** English language learners communicate information, ideas and concepts necessary for academic success in the content area of language arts.

About the Author—Lois Lowry

Lois Lowry was born on March 20, 1937, in Honolulu, Hawaii. However, because her father was in the military, she lived all over the world, including New York City, Pennsylvania, Washington, D.C., and Tokyo. She married a Naval officer while in college and followed her husband until he left the service and entered law school. As she raised their four children, she held onto her dream of becoming a writer, eventually returning to college and attending graduate school.

With her second husband, Lois Lowry has continued seeing the world, although she says that she is just as happy being home in Cambridge, Massachusetts. Although she has received many awards for her novels, she has also faced personal heartbreak. Her older son died while serving as a fighter pilot in the United States Air Force. Lowry is quoted as saying that the loss of her son "permeates her being" and that loss permeates *Son* as well (see Possible Texts for Text Comparisons). As a grandmother, she believes that "we live intertwined on this planet and that our future depends upon our caring more, and doing more, for one another."

Lowry has received two Newbery Awards, for *Number the Stars* and for *The Giver*. In her acceptance speech for *Number the Stars*, she describes how she learned many details for the novel from her close friend, Annelise. You can read the speech and learn more about Ms. Lowry at her website **http://www.loislowry.com/**.

Possible Texts for Text Comparisons

Looking Back: A Book of Memories provides insights into Lois Lowry's writing. *The Giver* is the first in a series of four novels that tackles difficult choices in a seemingly utopian world of the future. Other novels in the series include: *Gathering Blue*, *Messenger*, and *Son*.

Book Summary of *Number the Stars*

When Annemarie, Ellen, and Kirsti are stopped by German soldiers in the streets of Copenhagen, they have no idea how their lives are about to change. As news of the German's plans to relocate the Jewish people of Denmark leaks out, Annemarie's family joins others to ensure the safety of Ellen's family and other Jewish friends.

Ellen blends in with Annemarie's family during a harrowing visit from the soldiers in search of hidden Jewish people. Then the family takes Ellen to the seacoast to Uncle Henrik's house. A mock funeral is held as a way to deflect suspicion during a gathering of people, all of whom are bound for Sweden and safety. Ellen and her family are taken to Uncle Henrik's fishing boat and concealed in a hidden compartment for the journey. Meanwhile, Annemarie's mother is accidentally injured, and Annemarie must deliver a critical packet to Uncle Henrik—thus facing another encounter with the German soldiers.

Personal courage, fidelity, and loss are explored in the course of the story. Although the family is fictional, the story upon which it is based is true. The novel describes the remarkable success of a small country that saved more than 7,000 Jewish people in a matter of weeks.

Cross-Curricular Connection

This novel is appropriate for social studies, history, and literature studies. Specifically, this novel can be used during a study of World War II and the Holocaust.

Possible Texts for Text Sets

- Hesse, Karen. *Letters from Rifka*. Holt, 1992.
- Kerr, Judith. *When Hitler Stole Pink Rabbit*. Putnam, 1997.
- McSwigan, Marie. *Snow Treasure*. Puffin, 2006
- Yolen, Jane. *The Devil's Arithmetic*. Puffin, 1990.

Name _____

Date _____

Pre-Reading Theme Thoughts

Directions: Read each of the statements in the first column. Decide if you agree or disagree with the statements. Record your opinion by marking an X in Agree or Disagree for each statement. Explain your choices in the fourth column. There are no right or wrong answers.

Statement	Agree	Disagree	Explain Your Answer
Adults should always tell children the whole truth.			
Adults should not put children at risk, especially during times of war.			
You have to be brave and strong to save someone's life.			
During a war, it's best to focus on protecting yourself and your family instead of risking your family to help others.			

Vocabulary Overview

Ten key words from this section are provided below with definitions and sentences about how the words are used in the novel. Choose one of the vocabulary activity sheets (pages 15 or 16) for students to complete as they read this section. Monitor students as they work to ensure the definitions they have found are accurate and relate to the text. Finally, discuss these important vocabulary words with students. If you think these words or other words in the section warrant more time devoted to them, there are suggestions in the introduction for other vocabulary activities (page 5).

Word	Definition	Sentence about Text
obstinate (ch. 1)	stubborn	Annemarie hopes her **obstinate** sister will obey the soldiers.
impassive (ch. 1)	blank	The soldier is **impassive**, not looking at anything.
intricate (ch. 2)	complicated	Mama can make **intricate** and complex trimmings for clothes.
swastika (ch. 3)	Greek cross symbol	The soldiers wear the sign of the Nazi **swastika**.
curfew (ch. 3)	deadline	During the war, people have to be home before the 8:00 **curfew**.
sophisticated (ch. 4)	refined	Ellen speaks in a **sophisticated** voice, just like a fine actress.
glowering (ch. 4)	angry	Kirsti's **glowering** face shows that she is upset.
disdainfully (ch. 4)	scornfully	She puts away the shoes **disdainfully**, still upset.
belligerently (ch. 4)	aggressively	Kirsti argues back, talking **belligerently** about what she saw.
synagogue (ch. 4)	Jewish place of worship	The Rosen family wears their best clothes to worship at the **synagogue**.

Name _____

Date _____

Understanding Vocabulary Words

Directions: The following words appear in this section of the novel. Use context clues and reference materials to determine an accurate definition for each word.

Word	Definition
obstinate (ch. 1)	
impassive (ch. 1)	
intricate (ch. 2)	
swastika (ch. 3)	
curfew (ch. 3)	
sophisticated (ch. 4)	
glowering (ch. 4)	
disdainfully (ch. 4)	
belligerently (ch. 4)	
synagogue (ch. 4)	

Name _____

Date _____

During-Reading Vocabulary Activity

Directions: As you read these chapters, record at least eight important words on the lines below. Try to find interesting, difficult, intriguing, special, or funny words. Your words can be long or short. They can be hard or easy to spell. After each word, use context clues in the text and reference materials to define the word.

- _____

- _____

- _____

- _____

- _____

- _____

- _____

- _____

- _____

- _____

Directions: Respond to these questions about the words in this section.

1. Annemarie thinks about the German soldiers with **contempt**. Why does she feel this way?

   _____

   _____

2. Kirsti is **exasperated** when she gets new shoes. What does this tell you about Kirsti?

   _____

   _____

Analyzing the Literature

Provided below are discussion questions you can use in small groups, with the whole class, or for written assignments. Each question is given at two levels so you can choose the right question for each group of students. Activity sheets with these questions are provided (pages 18–19) if you want students to write their responses. For each question, a few key discussion points are provided for your reference.

Story Element	■ Level 1	▲ Level 2	Key Discussion Points
Plot	Why are the girls running on their way home from school?	Why do the soldiers stop the girls from running? What does the soldiers' behavior tell you about the Nazis?	The girls are running to practice racing. The soldiers say that they look like hoodlums and should not run. However, it is likely that they stop the girls just to bully and intimidate them.
Setting	Describe what Annemarie's neighborhood is like.	Describe the impact of having soldiers patrolling Annemarie's neighborhood.	Copenhagen is a large city. Annemarie lives in an apartment building, along with Ellen's family, the Rosens. During the discussion, talk about how unnerving it can be to be living in an occupied city. Draw comparisons to other places in the world where there is ongoing occupation or unrest.
Character	What activities keep Kirsti and Annemarie protected from the truth about the war?	Describe how the family protects Annemarie and Kirsti from what is happening with the war.	The girls read, tell stories, play together, and attend school. The family protects the girls by telling them limited information about what is happening and by continuing to do the activities the family has always done, such as telling fairy tales.
Plot	Why does Ellen stay with Annemarie at the end of chapter 4?	Explain why Ellen can't be told where her parents are. How would you feel if you were Ellen?	The family will pretend to have Ellen as part of their family if the soldiers come. If Ellen knows where her parents are, she could be put at risk if threatened or questioned. Ellen must feel worried and frightened.

Name _____

Date _____

■ Analyzing the Literature

Directions: Think about the section you just read. Read each question and state your response with textual evidence.

1. Why are the girls running on their way home from school?

_____

_____

_____

_____

2. Describe what Annemarie's neighborhood is like.

_____

_____

_____

_____

3. What activities keep Kirsti and Annemarie protected from the truth about the war?

_____

_____

_____

_____

4. Why does Ellen stay with Annemarie at the end of chapter 4?

_____

_____

_____

_____

Name _____

Date _____

▲ Analyzing the Literature

Directions: Think about the section you just read. Read each question and state your response with textual evidence.

1. Why do the soldiers stop the girls from running? What does the soldiers' behavior tell you about the Nazis?

    _____

    _____

    _____

2. Describe the impact of having soldiers patrolling in Annemarie's neighborhood.

    _____

    _____

    _____

3. Descibe how the family protects Annemarie and Kirsti from what is happening with the war.

    _____

    _____

    _____

    _____

4. Explain why Ellen can't be told where her parents are. How would you feel if you were Ellen?

    _____

    _____

    _____

    _____

Name _____

Date _____

Reader Response

Directions: Choose one of the following prompts about this section to answer. Be sure you include a topic sentence in your response, use textual evidence to support your opinion, and provide a strong conclusion that summarizes your opinion.

Writing Prompts

- **Opinion/Argument Piece**—The Rosens protect Ellen by leaving her. Describe a time when your parents kept something from you for your own good. Were they right to do so, or should they have been honest from the beginning?
- **Narrative Piece**—Think about what you know about the two families, the soldiers, and other things that you have read about World War II. Describe three different directions the plot could go at this point.

_____

_____

_____

_____

_____

_____

_____

_____

_____

_____

_____

_____

_____

_____

_____

Name _____

Date _____

Close Reading the Literature

Directions: Closely reread the first seven paragraphs of chapter 3. Read each question and then revisit the text to find evidence that supports your answer.

1. How is the walk to school different now? Why has it changed? Give text evidence to support your conclusion.

   _____

   _____

   _____

2. Use the text to explain why the mothers are knitting mittens and installing a little stove.

   _____

   _____

   _____

3. Use the novel to tell what the family does when they have no electricity.

   _____

   _____

   _____

4. Use the novel to explain why Annemarie is fearful she has said the wrong thing when she talks to her mother about the days when Kirsti used to sleep in Mama and Papa's room.

   _____

   _____

   _____

   _____

Name _____

Date _____

Making Connections—Where in the World?

Directions: Find a map of Europe in an atlas or on the Internet. Use the space below to draw Denmark. Show the following key areas: Copenhagen, the border with Germany, and the western boundary of Sweden. Save your map for reference as you read the rest of the novel.

Name _____

Date _____

Creating with the Story Elements

Directions: Thinking about the story elements of character, setting, and plot in a novel is very important to understanding what is happening and why. Complete **one** of the following activities based on what you've read so far. Be creative and have fun!

Characters

Create a character map for one character in the story. Make a circle in the center of your page with the character's name. Draw four connected circles around it. Label each connected circle with a heading: Description, Feelings, Personality Traits, and Actions. Add details from the novel in each circle.

Setting

How would you change your home so that you could cope with having no electricity or heat? Make a list of suggested tips. Or draw a picture of your home, and label places where you could make changes.

Plot

Write an article for the underground newspaper. Encourage the Danes to resist the Nazis. What actions could children take that would not put them at great risk? This is a good time to be extra clever!

Vocabulary Overview

Ten key words from this section are provided below with definitions and sentences about how the words are used in the novel. Choose one of the vocabulary activity sheets (pages 25 or 26) for students to complete as they read this section. Monitor students as they work to ensure the definitions they have found are accurate and relate to the text. Finally, discuss these important vocabulary words with students. If you think these words or other words in the section warrant more time devoted to them, there are suggestions in the introduction for other vocabulary activities (page 5).

Word	Definition	Sentence about Text
threatening (ch. 5)	bullying	The soldiers are always **threatening** people just so they can scare them.
intoned (ch. 5)	spoke	Ellen, who wants to be an actress, **intones** dramatically.
contentedly (ch. 5)	happily	Annemarie looks at her friend **contentedly** and falls asleep.
stalk (ch. 5)	stomp	The soldiers **stalk** across the room in their black boots.
frantically (ch. 5)	anxiously	Ellen pulls at the necklace **frantically**, trying to get it off.
clenched (ch. 5)	clasped	Annemarie looks at her **clenched** fingers that are holding the necklace.
tentatively (ch. 6)	hesitantly	The soldiers leave and the girls smile **tentatively**.
flower-sprigged (ch. 7)	decorated with flowers	Mama packs a **flower-sprigged** nightgown for Ellen to wear.
ruefully (ch. 8)	sorrowfully	Mama laughs **ruefully** at the rather sad joke.
specter (ch. 8)	threat, image of danger	The **specter** of soldiers with their frightful guns feels like a ghost story.

Understanding Vocabulary Words

Directions: The following words appear in this section of the novel. Use context clues and reference materials to determine an accurate definition for each word.

Word	Definition
threatening (ch. 5)	
intoned (ch. 5)	
contentedly (ch. 5)	
stalk (ch. 5)	
frantically (ch. 5)	
clenched (ch. 5)	
tentatively (ch. 6)	
flower-sprigged (ch. 7)	
ruefully (ch. 8)	
specter (ch. 8)	

Name _____

Date _____

During-Reading Vocabulary Activity

Directions: As you read these chapters, record at least eight important words on the lines below. Try to find interesting, difficult, intriguing, special, or funny words. Your words can be long or short. They can be hard or easy to spell. After each word, use context clues in the text and reference materials to define the word.

- _____

- _____

- _____

- _____

- _____

- _____

- _____

- _____

- _____

- _____

Directions: Respond to these questions about the words in this section.

1. In chapter 5, what is the purpose of the **blackout curtains** on the windows?

   _____

   _____

2. In chapter 8, why does Uncle Henrik shake his head in **mock dismay** at Mama's comment about him needing a wife?

   _____

   _____

Analyzing the Literature

Provided below are discussion questions you can use in small groups, with the whole class, or for written assignments. Each question is given at two levels so you can choose the right question for each group of students. Activity sheets with these questions are provided (pages 28–29) if you want students to write their responses. For each question, a few key discussion points are provided for your reference.

Story Element	■ Level 1	▲ Level 2	Key Discussion Points
Character	Where are Lise's things kept since her death?	Why do you think Lise's parents have kept her things since her death?	Lise's belongings, including her wedding dress, are kept in a blue trunk in Annemarie's room. Her parents are probably still grieving, unable to dispose of her belongings. Another reason could be practical—they could one day be used by Annemarie or Kirsti.
Plot	What does Annemarie hide to protect Ellen when the soldiers arrive?	How do Annemarie and her parents ensure Ellen's safety when the soldiers arrive?	Annemarie pulls off Ellen's necklace with its Star of David symbol. They all insist that Ellen is a member of the family, and Father uses pictures of Lise as a baby to support the story.
Setting	Describe the trip to Uncle Henrik's farm.	Why is the trip to Uncle Henrik's farm especially new and exciting for Ellen?	The train ride goes along the Danish coast, a beautiful route. Ellen has never seen the seacoast. The air is lovely and fresh, and they also walk through some woods to get there.
Character	How does Mama tease Uncle Henrik?	Why does Mama tease Uncle Henrik so much? How does he respond to Mama's teasing?	Mama insists that Uncle Henrik needs a wife. The house is dusty and she has to clean a lot. He laughs at her teasing, knowing that it is good-natured. Teasing between these siblings is clearly a very normal behavior in an abnormal time. It's helping to keep everyone calm.

Name _____

Date _____

Analyzing the Literature

Directions: Think about the section you just read. Read each question and state your response with textual evidence.

1. Where are Lise's things kept since her death?

_____

_____

_____

_____

2. What does Annemarie hide to protect Ellen when the soldiers arrive?

_____

_____

_____

_____

3. Describe the trip to Uncle Henrik's farm.

_____

_____

_____

_____

4. How does Mama tease Uncle Henrik?

_____

_____

_____

_____

Name _____

Date _____

▲ Analyzing the Literature

Directions: Think about the section you just read. Read each question and state your response with textual evidence.

1. Why do you think Lise's parents have kept all of her things since her death?

   _____

   _____

   _____

   _____

2. How do Annemarie and her parents ensure Ellen's safety when the soldiers arrive?

   _____

   _____

   _____

   _____

3. Why is the trip to Uncle Henrik's farm especially new and exciting for Ellen?

   _____

   _____

   _____

   _____

4. Why does Mama tease Uncle Henrik so much? How does he respond to Mama's teasing?

   _____

   _____

   _____

Name _____

Date _____

Reader Response

Directions: Choose one of the following prompts about this section to answer. Be sure you include a topic sentence in your response, use textual evidence to support your opinion, and provide a strong conclusion that summarizes your opinion.

Writing Prompts

- **Narrative Piece**—Consider the decisions, feelings, and challenges each character faces in this section. Which character can you relate to the most? Explain why you can relate to that character's experiences and feelings.
- **Informative/Explanatory Piece**—When soldiers visit in the middle of the night, they are suspicious about Ellen. Explain why they are suspicious and how Papa acts quickly to ensure Ellen's safety.

_____

_____

_____

_____

_____

_____

_____

_____

_____

_____

_____

_____

Close Reading the Literature

Directions: Closely reread the first twelve paragraphs of chapter 7, ending with "They giggled and stepped back." Read each question and then revisit the text to find evidence that supports your answer.

1. Annemarie discovers something about the house and meadows because Ellen is there. Explain what she discovers, using evidence from the text.

   _____

   _____

   _____

2. Find evidence in the text that supports the conclusion that the farmhouse is old.

   _____

   _____

   _____

3. Based on the events in this passage, describe the kitten's behavior.

   _____

   _____

   _____

4. Why does Ellen think of this sea differently from the harbor in Copenhagen? Include support to tell how Mrs. Rosen feels about the sea.

   _____

   _____

   _____

   _____

Name _____

Date _____

Making Connections–Out of Sight

Directions: Ellen hid in plain sight with Annemarie and her family. How would you hide a friend to be out of sight if you had to? Think about other novels you have read about the Holocaust or World War II and how people sometimes hid Jewish people. Choose a likely place in your home to hide a friend. You might build a false wall, hide a room behind bookshelves, or use space in an attic, basement, below the floorboards, underground, etc.

Describe your plan here:

_____

_____

_____

_____

_____

_____

_____

_____

_____

_____

_____

_____

_____

_____

_____

Extra challenge: Create a model of your design. Use a shoebox, blocks, craft sticks, or other materials for your model.

Name _____

Date _____

Creating with the Story Elements

Directions: Thinking about the story elements of character, setting, and plot in a novel is very important to understanding what is happening and why. Complete **one** of the following activities based on what you've read so far. Be creative and have fun!

Characters

Create an advertisement to recruit Resistance fighters. It should describe the necessary characteristics to fill this role. Think about the various roles that all ages and both genders could take on. Make your advertisement detailed and inspirational.

Setting

Create a model of Uncle Henrik's charming farmhouse and grounds based on the description in this section. Use a choice of media, such as watercolors, that can capture the beauty of the area.

Plot

Create a problem-solution story map. Identify four problems, such as the Nazis making lists of the Jewish people. Write one problem in a box, and write the solution in a corresponding box. Connect each set with arrows to indicate the progress of the plot.

Vocabulary Overview

Ten key words from this section are provided below with definitions and sentences about how the words are used in the novel. Choose one of the vocabulary activity sheets (pages 35 or 36) for students to complete as they read this section. Monitor students as they work to ensure the definitions they have found are accurate and relate to the text. Finally, discuss these important vocabulary words with students. If you think these words or other words in the section warrant more time devoted to them, there are suggestions in the introduction for other vocabulary activities (page 5).

Word	Definition	Sentence about Text
poised (ch. 9)	perched	The cat sits nearby, **poised** and ready to pounce.
deftly (ch. 9)	skillfully	Uncle Henrik **deftly** milks the cow with his strong hands.
frothy (ch. 9)	foamy	The fresh milk is **frothy** on top, nearly filling the bucket.
determined (ch. 9)	strong-minded	Uncle Henrik tells Annemarie that she is like him—**determined** to do the right thing.
urgency (ch. 9)	pressure; stress	This time, Peter says goodbye with a sense of **urgency** and worry.
recurring (ch. 10)	repeating	Annemarie hears the soldiers' boots again. It feels like a **recurring** nightmare.
staccato (ch. 10)	short; clipped	The boots make that same **staccato** beat on the floor.
condescending (ch. 10)	sneering; put-down	The soldier pretends to be sad about the death. He uses a **condescending** voice.
extinguished (ch. 10)	snuffed; dowsed	After the soldiers leave, Peter relights the **extinguished** candle.
distribute (ch. 11)	hand out	Peter begins to **distribute** the coats to the waiting people.

Name _____

Date _____

Understanding Vocabulary Words

Directions: The following words appear in this section of the novel. Use context clues and reference materials to determine an accurate definition for each word.

Word	Definition
poised (ch. 9)	
deftly (ch. 9)	
frothy (ch. 9)	
determined (ch. 9)	
urgency (ch. 9)	
recurring (ch. 10)	
staccato (ch. 10)	
condescending (ch. 10)	
extinguished (ch. 10)	
distribute (ch. 11)	

Name _____

Date _____

During-Reading Vocabulary Activity

Directions: As you read these chapters, record at least eight important words on the lines below. Try to find interesting, difficult, intriguing, special, or funny words. Your words can be long or short. They can be hard or easy to spell. After each word, use context clues in the text and reference materials to define the word.

- _____
- _____
- _____
- _____
- _____
- _____
- _____
- _____
- _____
- _____

Directions: Now, organize your words. Rewrite each of your words on a sticky note. Work as a group to create a bar graph of your words. You should stack any words that are the same on top of one another. Different words appear in different columns. Finally, discuss with a group why certain words were chosen more often than other words.

Analyzing the Literature

Provided below are discussion questions you can use in small groups, with the whole class, or for written assignments. Each question is given at two levels so you can choose the right question for each group of students. Activity sheets with these questions are provided (pages 38–39) if you want students to write their responses. For each question, a few key discussion points are provided for your reference.

Story Element	■ Level 1	▲ Level 2	Key Discussion Points
Plot	What is the lie about Great-aunt Birte?	Why do they lie about Great-aunt Birte? Do you think Mama is right to lie to Annemarie? Why or why not?	There is no Great-aunt Birte. A funeral is an excuse to have a gathering of people, and Mama wants to protect the girls. Opinions may vary as to whether that is the right choice.
Character	Why does Annemarie lie to Ellen when she pretends she really has a dead aunt?	How do Annemarie and her mother come to be "equals" during the pretend funeral for Great-aunt Birte?	Annemarie wants to protect Ellen from the truth to help keep her safe. Annemarie and her mother recognize the importance of keeping the lie alive for everyone's benefit.
Plot	How is Ellen reunited with her parents?	How does the reunion with Ellen's parents change the relationship between Ellen and Annemarie?	Ellen's parents have been brought to the gathering. Annemarie recognizes that Ellen and she will face different challenges and a different world, which saddens her.
Setting	The soldiers want to open the casket to see the body. How is this stopped?	How do they trick the soldiers into leaving? Why is it a relief that the casket was not opened?	They tell the soldiers that Great-aunt Birte died of typhus and act like they will open the casket. If the soldiers saw the blankets and clothing inside the casket, they would have found out about the escape plan.

Name _____

Date _____

■ Analyzing the Literature

Directions: Think about the section you just read. Read each question and state your response with textual evidence.

1. What is the lie about Great-aunt Birte?

_____

_____

_____

_____

2. Why does Annemarie lie to Ellen when she pretends she really has a dead aunt?

_____

_____

_____

_____

3. How is Ellen reunited with her parents?

_____

_____

_____

_____

4. The soldiers want to open the casket to see the body. How is this stopped?

_____

_____

_____

_____

▲ Analyzing the Literature

Directions: Think about the section you just read. Read each question and state your response with textual evidence.

1. Why do they lie about Great-aunt Birte? Do you think Mama is right to lie to Annemarie? Why or why not?

   _____

   _____

   _____

2. How do Annemarie and her mother come to be "equals" during the pretend funeral for Great-aunt Birte?

   _____

   _____

   _____

3. How does the reunion with Ellen's parents change the relationship between Ellen and Annemarie?

   _____

   _____

   _____

   _____

4. How do they trick the soldiers into leaving? Why is it a relief that the casket was not opened?

   _____

   _____

   _____

   _____

Name _____

Date _____

Reader Response

Directions: Choose one of the following prompts about this section to answer. Be sure you include a topic sentence in your response, use textual evidence to support your opinion, and provide a strong conclusion that summarizes your opinion.

Writing Prompts

- **Opinion/Argument Piece**—Ellen is leaving, and Annemarie is staying behind. It is likely that the friends will not see each other for a long time. Which situation would be more difficult for you—leaving or staying behind? Explain why and how you would feel.

- **Informative/Explanatory Piece**—Explain the preparations for the people leaving with Uncle Henrik. Predict how they will be hidden. Also, make a prediction about the importance of the packet and why Peter has not explained what is inside.

_____

_____

_____

_____

_____

_____

_____

_____

_____

_____

_____

Name _____

Date _____

Close Reading the Literature

Directions: Closely reread the last six paragraphs of chapter 11. Read each question and then revisit the text to find evidence that supports your answer.

1. The text says, "It was an odd word: pride." Describe why Annemarie thinks the word pride is odd. Support your claim with evidence from the text.

    _____

    _____

    _____

2. Give examples from the text of symbols of pride that the Rosens leave behind.

    _____

    _____

    _____

3. Use text evidence to explain what fears each of the Rosens have.

    _____

    _____

    _____

    _____

4. Give evidence from the text to tell what Annemarie sees to show that the Rosens still have their pride.

    _____

    _____

    _____

    _____

Name _____

Date _____

Making Connections—
Denmark to Sweden by Boat

In September 1943, the Danish Resistance was told that the Jewish people were to be deported. This is what happened next:

- More than 7,000 Jewish people were smuggled to the coast.
- Next they were taken to Sweden across the cold, choppy water.
- The Jewish people were moved in fishing boats, rowboats, and even kayaks!
- Each trip in a fishing boat took about an hour at night. It took longer in rowboats and kayaks.
- The entire rescue effort took about three weeks.

Directions: Read the information and answer the questions.

- You have a fishing boat.
- You make two round trips on your fishing boat each night.
- You have five people on your boat for each trip.

1. How many people can you smuggle into Sweden in one night? _____

2. How many people can you smuggle into Sweden in one week? _____

3. How many people can you smuggle into Sweden in two weeks? _____

4. How many people can you smuggle into Sweden in five weeks? _____

5. You need to save 7,350 people in a week. How many fishing boats do you need? Assume each boat can hold five people and takes two round trips each night. _____

Creating with the Story Elements

Directions: Thinking about the story elements of character, setting, and plot in a novel is very important to understanding what is happening and why. Complete **one** of the following activities based on what you've read so far. Be creative and have fun!

Characters

Think about the effects of the war on Ellen. Make a chart that lists the effects of war in the following categories: Friendships, Family Life, Future (hopes and dreams), and Basic Needs (food, clothing, shelter).

Setting

Draw a picture of the people trying to find their way to the boat in the dark. Think about the description of the path, the woods, and what they had to carry. Make your drawing show the dangers and the emotions they must feel.

Plot

This section ends with Annemarie realizing that her mother is injured. This kind of plot device is called a cliffhanger. It makes the reader want to find out what happened to her and what will happen next. Make a graphic organizer that shows two events that might have led up to the cliffhanger. Show the cliffhanger in the center. Then show two possible events that could happen next.

Vocabulary Overview

Ten key words from this section are provided below with definitions and sentences about how the words are used in the novel. Choose one of the vocabulary activity sheets (pages 45 or 46) for students to complete as they read this section. Monitor students as they work to ensure the definitions they have found are accurate and relate to the text. Finally, discuss these important vocabulary words with students. If you think these words or other words in the section warrant more time devoted to them, there are suggestions in the introduction for other vocabulary activities (page 5).

Word	Definition	Sentence about Text
hobbled (ch. 13)	limped	Annemarie helps while Mama tries to **hobble** back home.
stricken (ch. 13)	troubled	Mama's face looks **stricken** when she realizes Uncle Henrik didn't get the packet.
bulky (ch. 14)	thick	The people look **bulky** in their padded clothes.
vivid (ch. 14)	intense	Kirsti's **vivid** imagination makes stories come alive.
prolong (ch. 14)	lengthen	Annemarie likes to **prolong** the story for Kirsti.
tantalize (ch. 14)	tease; torment	Annemarie likes to **tantalize** Kirsti, building up the suspense in stories.
taut (ch. 14)	tight	Annemarie stops when she sees the soldiers. Two dogs pull at their **taut** leashes.
withering (ch. 15)	dismissive	Annemarie looks at the soldier in disbelief and gives him a **withering** look.
insolently (ch. 15)	rudely	Annemarie speaks **insolently** to the soldiers as part of her plan.
contempt (ch. 15)	dislike	The soldier speaks to her with **contempt** as he scolds her.

Name _____

Date _____

Understanding Vocabulary Words

Directions: The following words appear in this section of the novel. Use context clues and reference materials to determine an accurate definition for each word.

Word	Definition
hobbled (ch. 13)	
stricken (ch. 13)	
bulky (ch. 14)	
vivid (ch. 14)	
prolong (ch. 14)	
tantalize (ch. 14)	
taut (ch. 14)	
withering (ch. 15)	
insolently (ch. 15)	
contempt (ch. 15)	

Name _____

Date _____

During-Reading Vocabulary Activity

Directions: As you read these chapters, record at least eight important words on the lines below. Try to find interesting, difficult, intriguing, special, or funny words. Your words can be long or short. They can be hard or easy to spell. After each word, use context clues in the text and reference materials to define the word.

- _____
- _____
- _____
- _____
- _____
- _____
- _____
- _____
- _____
- _____

Directions: Respond to these questions about the words in this section.

1. In chapter 14, the older doctor is a **brusque** man. How does he act?

    _____

    _____

2. At the end of chapter 15, Annemarie hands over the basket to her uncle. She has been brave, but now her voice is **quavering**. Why does her voice quaver?

    _____

    _____

Analyzing the Literature

Provided below are discussion questions you can use in small groups, with the whole class, or for written assignments. Each question is given at two levels so you can choose the right question for each group of students. Activity sheets with these questions are provided (pages 48–49) if you want students to write their responses. For each question, a few key discussion points are provided for your reference.

Story Element	■ Level 1	▲ Level 2	Key Discussion Points
Plot	What has happened to Mama?	How does Mama's injury affect the plan?	Mama trips on the path and hurts her leg. Annemarie has to get the packet to her uncle.
Setting	How does Annemarie keep herself from getting too scared when going through the woods?	Compare Annemarie's thoughts about Little Red Riding Hood in the woods with the true dangers she faces.	Annemarie thinks about getting through the woods, just like Little Red Riding Hood. The primary danger is that of the soldiers. They and their dogs can be compared to the Big Bad Wolf.
Character	How does Annemarie act toward the soldiers?	What works and what doesn't with Annemarie's act for the soldiers?	She acts like a bratty child. Her act hides her fear from the soldiers. However, the dogs continue to focus on the basket, and the soldiers end up looking through the contents of the basket. Annemarie thinks they are going to discover something important, but the men don't regard the handkerchief as a threat.
Plot	How does Uncle Henrik react to Annemarie's arrival?	Why has Annemarie's arrival relieved Uncle Henrik's fears?	Uncle Henrik is worried when he sees her, then relieved when he examines the basket. His fears are relieved because she brought the packet. For whatever reason, the handkerchief is important to the escape plan.

Name _____

Date _____

■ Analyzing the Literature

Directions: Think about the section you just read. Read each question and state your response with textual evidence.

1. What has happened to Mama?

_____

_____

_____

_____

2. How does Annemarie keep herself from getting too scared when going through the woods?

_____

_____

_____

_____

3. How does Annemarie act toward the soldiers?

_____

_____

_____

_____

4. How does Uncle Henrik react to Annemarie's arrival?

_____

_____

_____

_____

Name _____

Date _____

▲ Analyzing the Literature

Directions: Think about the section you just read. Read each question and state your response with textual evidence.

1. How does Mama's injury affect the plan?

_____

_____

_____

_____

2. Compare Annemarie's thoughts about Little Red Riding Hood in the woods with the true dangers she faces.

_____

_____

_____

_____

3. What works and what doesn't with Annemarie's act for the soldiers?

_____

_____

_____

_____

4. Why has Annemarie's arrival relieved Uncle Henrik's fears?

_____

_____

_____

_____

Name _____

Date _____

Reader Response

Directions: Choose one of the following prompts about this section to answer. Be sure you include a topic sentence in your response, use textual evidence to support your opinion, and provide a strong conclusion that summarizes your opinion.

Writing Prompts

- **Narrative Piece**—Annemarie thinks about Kirsti when she faces the soldiers in the woods. When have you thought about a sibling or friend in a tough situation? Compare it to Annemarie's challenge.
- **Informative/Explanatory Piece**—Think about what you know about the Resistance effort so far. Write at least two questions about the Resistance effort, and explain why you are curious about the answers.

_____

_____

_____

_____

_____

_____

_____

_____

_____

_____

_____

_____

_____

Close Reading the Literature

Directions: Closely reread the first half of chapter 15. Read from the beginning of the chapter through the paragraph that says, "Please, please, she implored in her mind. Don't lift the napkin." Read each question and then revisit the text to find evidence that supports your answer.

1. Acting like Kirsti helps Annemarie face the soldiers. Describe two examples of how Kirsti previously acted around soldiers.

   _____

   _____

   _____

2. What textual details tell you that the soldiers' dogs are dangerous?

   _____

   _____

   _____

3. Give examples from the passage that show how Annemarie chatters like Kirsti.

   _____

   _____

   _____

4. According to the text, why should the soldier know that Annemarie does not have any meat in the basket?

   _____

   _____

   _____

Name _____

Date _____

Making Connections–Taking Sides

Directions: Some countries, like Denmark, were occupied by the Germans. Some countries were neutral. Others fought against the Germans. Use a map to locate Germany and shade it blue. Then, shade the occupied countries red and shade the neutral countries green.

Nazi Occupied Countries		Neutral Countries
Albania	Latvia	Ireland
Austria	Lithuania	Portugal
Belgium	Luxembourg	Spain
Czechoslovakia	The Netherlands	Sweden
Denmark	Norway	Switzerland
Estonia	Poland	Turkey
France	Yugoslavia	
Greece		

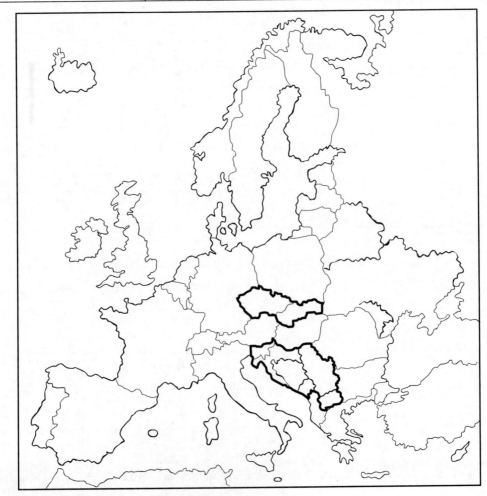

Name _____

Date _____

Creating with the Story Elements

Directions: Thinking about the story elements of character, setting, and plot in a novel is very important to understanding what is happening and why. Complete **one** of the following activities based on what you've read so far. Be creative and have fun!

Characters

Choose a hero from the characters in the novel. Make a poster that includes why this character is a hero.

Setting

Create a tableau of the scene where the soldiers are confronting Annemarie. Have classmates help by posing using props, or create the tableau with your family as actors and take a digital picture.

Plot

Create a plot map that shows the rising action of the story up through this section. It can look like a set of steps, a ladder, or a design of your choice. Label the key plot points.

Vocabulary Overview

Ten key words from this section are provided below with definitions and sentences about how the words are used in the novel. Choose one of the vocabulary activity sheets (pages 55 or 56) for students to complete as they read this section. Monitor students as they work to ensure the definitions they have found are accurate and relate to the text. Finally, discuss these important vocabulary words with students. If you think these words or other words in the section warrant more time devoted to them, there are suggestions in the introduction for other vocabulary activities (page 5).

Word	Definition	Sentence about Text
concealed (ch. 16)	hidden	Uncle Henrik explains how the Jewish people are **concealed** on his boat.
confronting (ch. 16)	threatening	Annemarie describes how the soldiers were **confronting** her on the path.
chatterbox (ch. 17)	someone who talks a lot	Kirsti is quieter now; no longer a **chatterbox**.
devastating (ch. 17)	upsetting	Learning of a death is **devastating** to the family.
executed (ch. 17)	killed	Finding out that a person was **executed** is even more distressing.
bleak (ch. 17)	dreary	The graves are **bleak**, with little more than dirt.
grief (ch. 17)	sadness	Memories of Lise fill Annemarie with **grief**.
deprivation (afterword)	scarcity	During wartime, people must get by and learn to live with **deprivation**.
compassion (afterword)	kindness	One person's **compassion** can make a big difference.
permeated (afterword)	soaked	The dogs are confused by the smell of the **permeated** handkerchief.

Name _____

Date _____

Understanding Vocabulary Words

Directions: The following words appear in this section of the novel. Use context clues and reference materials to determine an accurate definition for each word.

Word	Definition
concealed (ch. 16)	
confronting (ch. 16)	
chatterbox (ch. 17)	
devastating (ch. 17)	
executed (ch. 17)	
bleak (ch. 17)	
grief (ch. 17)	
deprivation (afterword)	
compassion (afterword)	
permeated (afterword)	

Name _____

Date _____

During-Reading Vocabulary Activity

Directions: As you read these chapters, choose five important words from the story. Use these words to complete the word flow chart below. On each arrow, write a word. In each box, explain how the connected pair of words relates to each other. An example for the words *grief* and *devastating* has been done for you.

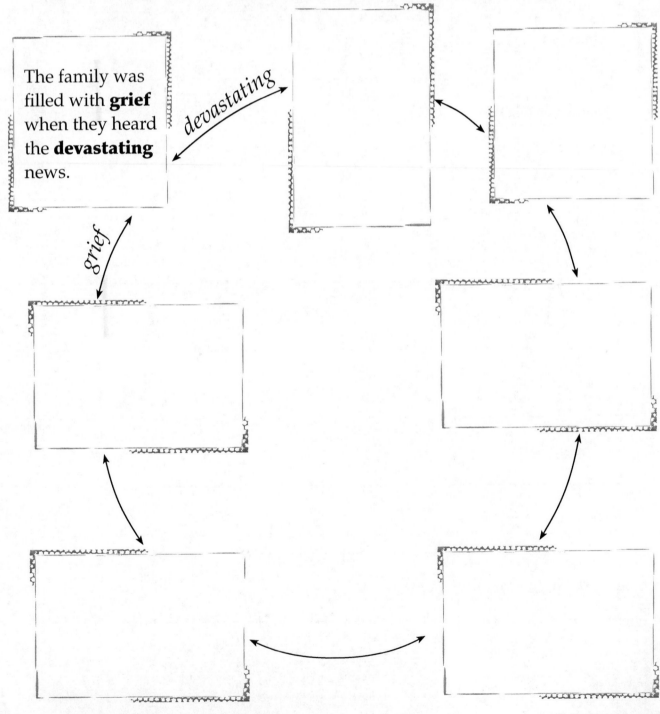

The family was filled with **grief** when they heard the **devastating** news.

devastating

grief

© Shell Education

Analyzing the Literature

Provided below are discussion questions you can use in small groups, with the whole class, or for written assignments. Each question is given at two levels so you can choose the right question for each group of students. Activity sheets with these questions are provided (pages 58–59) if you want students to write their responses. For each question, a few key discussion points are provided for your reference.

Story Element	■ Level 1	▲ Level 2	Key Discussion Points
Character	How does Uncle Henrik show bravery? How does Annemarie show bravery?	In what way is Annemarie as brave as Uncle Henrik?	Uncle Henrik shows bravery as he conceals the Jewish people in a compartment of the boat, hiding it with fish. Annemarie is brave because she focuses on delivering the packet despite her fears.
Plot	Why is the handkerchief so important?	Explain how the handkerchief works. Do you think they should have told Annemarie how it works before she took the basket to the boat?	The handkerchief is treated so that the dogs can't smell things normally. This is another example of how it is probably best for Annemarie to not fully understand the way they outwit the Germans.
Setting	What is the journey to Sweden like for the Rosens?	Explain why Sweden is the best place for the Rosens.	It is dark, cold, and cramped. Mrs. Rosen is seasick. But the air is fresh and cool in Sweden and the trip isn't long. Germany doesn't plan to invade Sweden. Therefore the Rosens can stay there safely until the end of the war.
Plot	What is the truth about Lise and her death?	Do you think the children should have been told the truth about Lise? Why or why not?	Lise was part of the Resistance and was hit by a military car as she tried to run from the Nazis. This is another example of how the whole truth could have been dangerous for the children to know.

Name _____

Date _____

Analyzing the Literature

Directions: Think about the section you just read. Read each question and state your response with textual evidence.

1. How does Uncle Henrik show bravery? How does Annemarie show bravery?

_____

_____

_____

_____

2. Why is the handkerchief so important?

_____

_____

_____

_____

3. What is the journey to Sweden like for the Rosens?

_____

_____

_____

_____

4. What is the truth about Lise and her death?

_____

_____

_____

_____

Name _____

Date _____

▲ Analyzing the Literature

Directions: Think about the section you just read. Read each question and state your response with textual evidence.

1. In what ways was Annemarie as brave as Uncle Henrik?

_____

_____

_____

_____

2. Explain how the handkerchief works. Do you think they should have told Annemarie how it works before she took the basket to the boat?

_____

_____

_____

_____

3. Explain why Sweden is the best place for the Rosens.

_____

_____

_____

_____

4. Do you think the children should have been told the truth about Lise? Why or why not?

_____

_____

_____

_____

Name _____

Date _____

Reader Response

Directions: Choose one of the following prompts about this section to answer. Be sure you include a topic sentence in your response, use textual evidence to support your opinion, and provide a strong conclusion that summarizes your opinion.

Writing Prompts

- **Opinion/Argument Piece**—Think about what you learn about Lise from the beginning of the novel to the end. Decide whether you would join the Resistance movement if you were Lise. Explain why or why not.
- **Narrative Piece**—Think about the conversation Annemarie and Ellen will have when they meet again. Think about what they will ask each other and tell each other. Write their conversation.

_____

_____

_____

_____

_____

_____

_____

_____

_____

_____

_____

_____

_____

Name _____

Date _____

Close Reading the Literature

Directions: Closely reread the first seven paragraphs of chapter 17. Read each question and then revisit the text to find evidence that supports your answer.

1. Give examples from the text of how the Danish people celebrate the end of the war.

   _____

   _____

   _____

2. Based on the text, how have the neighbors taken care of their Jewish friends who fled Denmark?

   _____

   _____

   _____

3. How has Kirsti changed? Find evidence to support this conclusion.

   _____

   _____

   _____

   _____

4. Use the novel to tell why the family is sad on such a happy day.

   _____

   _____

   _____

   _____

Name _____

Date _____

Making Connections–
Ten Commandments for Danes

The Danes knew that they could not fight off the Germans directly. But the Danish people could do other things to help defeat the Nazis. Arne Sejr was a young Danish man when the Germans invaded. He was very upset when people were friendly to the Germans. So, he created a list of Ten Commandments—or things to do to help stop the Germans.

Directions: Think about what you've read in this novel. Add five more commandments to the list. Consider adding commandments about food, shopping, etc.

1. You must not go to work in Germany.

2. You shall do a bad job for the Germans.

3. You shall work slowly for the Germans.

4. You shall delay all transport.

5. You shall treat traitors for what they are worth.

6. _____

7. _____

8. _____

9. _____

10. _____

Name _____

Date _____

Creating with the Story Elements

Directions: Thinking about the story elements of character, setting, and plot in a novel is very important to understanding what is happening and why. Complete **one** of the following activities based on what you've read so far. Be creative and have fun!

Characters

In chapter 17, you learn that Peter writes a letter to the family. Write Peter's letter. Include what the story says he wrote, adding anything else that you would write if you were Peter.

Setting

Make a drawing or painting of the apartment buildings on Annemarie's street as described in chapter 17. Research the appearance of the Danish flag to include in your artwork.

Plot

This novel mentions many symbols: pride, Nazis, Judaism, bravery, etc. Choose a symbol that you feel best represents the story, and create a representation of that symbol. It can be artistic, a slogan, a bumper sticker, a poem, or any other appropriate form.

Name _____

Date _____

Post-Reading Theme Thoughts

Directions: Read each of the statements in the first column. Choose a main character from *Number the Stars*. Think about that character's point of view. From that character's perspective, decide if the character would agree or disagree with the statements. Record the character's opinion by marking an *X* in Agree or Disagree for each statement. Explain your choices in the fourth column using text evidence.

Character I Chose: _____

Statement	Agree	Disagree	Explain Your Answer
Adults should always tell children the whole truth.			
Adults should not put children at risk, especially during times of war.			
You have to be brave and strong to save someone's life.			
During a war, it's best to focus on protecting yourself and your family instead of risking your family to help others.			

Name _____

Date _____

Culminating Activity: The Sequel

Directions: Think about the personalities of Ellen and Annemarie. They had hopes and dreams for their futures. Choose one of these two female characters. Think about the events of the war. Consider how some of these events may be positive while other events were negative. Complete the last box with realistic possibilities for the future.

Character

Events of the War

Positive Effects	Negative Effects

Possibilities for the Future

Name _____

Date _____

Culminating Activity: The Sequel (cont.)

Directions: Based on the chart you've completed, create a plan for your sequel to *Number the Stars*. Plan the characters, the setting, and the sequence of events. Think about how Lois Lowry paced the plot, with a series of rising action to the climax and falling action in the last two chapters.

Title			
Who?	**What?**	**When?**	**Where?**
Event 1			
Event 2			
Event 3			
Event 4			
Ending			

Name _____

Date _____

Comprehension Assessment

Directions: Circle the best response to each question.

1. What is the meaning of the word *sabotage* as it is used in chapter 1 of the novel?

    A. occupation

    B. disruption

    C. eavesdropping

    D. secretive

2. Which detail from the novel best supports your answer to question 1?

    E. "*De Frie Danske—The Free Danes*—was an illegal newspaper . . . ."

    F. "She told her mother and Mrs. Rosen of the incident, trying to make it look humorous and unimportant."

    G. "It is important to be one of the crowd, always."

    H. The Resistance fighters "were determined to bring harm to the Nazis however they could."

3. What is the main idea of the text below about the planned relocation of the Jewish people?

    > "The rabbi knew because a high German official told the Danish government, which passed the information along to the leaders of the Jewish community. The name of that German was G.F. Duckwitz, and I hope that even today, so many years later, there are flowers on his grave, because he was a man of compassion and courage."

    A. It's good to be a leader in a community.

    B. One man chose to do the right thing, no matter what the risk.

    C. Some Germans were ordinary soldiers, just doing their jobs.

    D. The Danish Resistance showed great courage.

4. Choose **two** supporting details for your answer to question 3.

    E. Most of the Jewish people believed the warning about the relocation.

    F. The handkerchief helped save the Jewish people because it confused the dogs.

    G. Jewish people observed the Jewish High Holidays in the synagogue.

    H. About seven thousand Jewish people were smuggled into Sweden.

Comprehension Assessment (cont.)

5. Which statement best expresses one of the themes of the novel?

    A. Some countries avoid war at any cost.

    B. Enemies should be forgiven.

    C. Close friends show they care during times of trouble.

    D. Tolerance can change the world.

6. What detail from the novel provides the best evidence for your answer to number 5?

    E. Peter is executed in the public square in Copenhagen.

    F. Sweden provided a refuge for the Jewish people.

    G. People wept in the streets when the war ended.

    H. People kept the Jewish people's apartments clean in their absence.

7. What is the purpose of this sentence written by a member of the Resistance in the afterword? ". . . but the dream for you all, young and old, must be to create an ideal of human decency, and not a narrow-minded and prejudiced one."

    _____

    _____

    _____

    _____

    _____

8. What other quotation from the story serves a similar purpose?

    A. "Surely that gift—the gift of a world of human decency—is the one that all countries hunger for still."

    B. "The secret operations that saved the Jews were orchestrated by the Danish Resistance . . . ."

    C. "The people would have been destroyed had they tried to defend themselves against the huge German forces."

    D. "Peter Nielsen, though he is fictional, represents those courageous and idealistic young people . . . ."

Name _____

Date _____

Response to Literature: Your Turn

Overview: Some adults think that kids should be protected from the realities of war. Some think that kids can't really do much to help. Although our country may not be at war all the time, there are difficult things that still happen. People of all ages are bullied. Some people don't have enough food to eat. Some people have to wear shabby clothes.

Directions: Think about what is happening in your community. What are the needs? What are kids doing to help, or what can kids do to help? Write an essay that describes the effect that kids can have to fix a problem or help people in need.

Write an essay that follows these guidelines:

- **State your opinion about something that kids can do to help people in need.**

- **Write at least 750 words.**

- **Include main points, such as why kids can help, how they can help, and how others have helped.**

- **Draw upon examples of things kids have done in your community or that you've read about.**

- **Provide a conclusion that summarizes your point of view.**

Name _____

Date _____

Response to Literature Rubric

Directions: Use this rubric to evaluate student responses.

	Exceptional Writing	Quality Writing	Developing Writing
Focus and Organization	☐ States a clear opinion and elaborates well. Engages the reader from the opening hook through the middle to the conclusion. Demonstrates clear understanding of the intended audience and purpose of the piece.	☐ Provides a clear and consistent opinion. Maintains a clear perspective and supports it through elaborating details. Makes the opinion clear in the opening hook and summarizes well in the conclusion.	☐ Provides an inconsistent point of view. Does not support the topic adequately or misses pertinent information. Provides lack of clarity in the beginning, middle, and conclusion.
Text Evidence	☐ Provides comprehensive and accurate support. Includes relevant and worthwhile text references.	☐ Provides limited support. Provides few supporting text references.	☐ Provides very limited support for the text. Provides no supporting text references.
Written Expression	☐ Uses descriptive and precise language with clarity and intention. Maintains a consistent voice and uses an appropriate tone that supports meaning. Uses multiple sentence types and transitions well between ideas.	☐ Uses a broad vocabulary. Maintains a consistent voice and supports a tone and feelings through language. Varies sentence length and word choices.	☐ Uses a limited and unvaried vocabulary. Provides an inconsistent or weak voice and tone. Provides little to no variation in sentence type and length.
Language Conventions	☐ Capitalizes, punctuates, and spells accurately. Demonstrates complete thoughts within sentences, with accurate subject-verb agreement. Uses paragraphs appropriately and with clear purpose.	☐ Capitalizes, punctuates, and spells accurately. Demonstrates complete thoughts within sentences and appropriate grammar. Paragraphs are properly divided and supported.	☐ Incorrectly capitalizes, punctuates, and spells. Uses fragmented or run-on sentences. Utilizes poor grammar overall. Paragraphs are poorly divided and developed.

During-Reading Vocabulary Activity—Section 1: Chapters 1–4 (page 16)

1. **Contempt** means dislike or disdain. Annemarie feels this way because the soldiers are mean, they haven't learned to speak Danish, and they sneer at the children.

2. Kirsti is frustrated and annoyed. She is young and doesn't fully understand the realities of the war.

Close Reading the Literature—Section 1: Chapters 1–4 (page 21)

1. The children must be cautious around the soldiers, making sure not to draw attention to themselves.

2. The fuel is gone, so they have to conserve what little coal they can find as winter approaches.

3. They burn candles for light and use the little stove when they find coal.

4. This is also the time when Annemarie shared a room with Lise. She worries she has reminded her mother about Lise's death.

During-Reading Vocabulary Activity—Section 2: Chapters 5–8 (page 26)

1. The **blackout curtains** prevent light from being seen from the outside. They keep the buildings from being seen by bombers.

2. **Mock dismay** means to pretend to be sad or upset. Uncle Henrik is mostly teasing back and keeping things light.

Close Reading the Literature—Section 2: Chapters 5–8 (page 31)

1. Annemarie sees the house and meadows with fresh eyes. She appreciates them because of Ellen's pleasure in their beauty.

2. The farmhouse has a crooked chimney and windows.

3. The kitten pounces on pretend mice, licks its paws, darts off, and is happy to have the girls around.

4. The sea is open, not like around Copenhagen. Mrs. Rosen is afraid, saying the ocean is too big and cold.

Close Reading the Literature—Section 3: Chapters 9–12 (page 41)

1. The people are wearing ill-fitting clothing, holding ragged blankets, and looking tired and humble—not displaying pride in their outward appearance.

2. They left behind candlesticks, books, and dreams of being in the theater.

3. Mrs. Rosen fears the sea—its width, depth, and cold. Ellen is frightened of the soldiers. They all are frightened of the future.

4. The Rosens' shoulders are still straight.

Making Connections—Section 3: Chapters 9–12 (page 42)

1. 10 people
2. 70 people
3. 140 people
4. 350 people
5. 105 fishing boats

During-Reading Vocabulary Activity—Section 4: Chapters 13–15 (page 46)

1. The doctor acts brisk and gruff.

2. She has had a frightening experience. She doesn't know if she has succeeded with what she needed to do until she sees her uncle's look of relief.

Close Reading the Literature—Section 4: Chapters 13–15 (page 51)

1. Kirsti is never frightened. She is silly. She knows nothing of danger.

2. The dogs are tense and alert. The soldiers are wearing thick gloves.

3. She talks about how Uncle Henrik doesn't like fish, wouldn't eat them raw unless starving, and always has bread and cheese.

4. The people of Denmark no longer have meat because the German Army eats all of it.

Making Connections—Section 4: Chapters 13–15 (page 52)

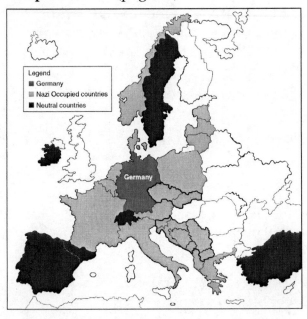

Legend
- Germany
- Nazi Occupied countries
- Neutral countries

Germany

Close Reading the Literature—Section 5: Chapters 16–17 (page 61)

1. The church bells ring that evening. The flag is raised and people weep as they sing the national anthem.

2. The neighbors have watered plants, dusted furniture, and polished candlesticks.

3. Kirsti is more serious, taller, and thin.

4. Peter Neilsen is captured by the Germans and executed.

Making Connections—Section 5: Chapters 16–17 (page 62)

1. Answers will vary, but could include commandments such as: destroy tools and machines, boycott German films and papers, not shop at the Nazi stores, protect anyone chased by the Germans, or destroy anything that would help the Germans.

Comprehension Assessment (pages 67–68)

1. B. disruption

2. H. The Resistance fighters "were determined to bring harm to the Nazis however they could."

3. B. One man chose to do the right thing, no matter what the risk.

4. E. Most of the Jewish people believed the warning about the relocation.
   H. About seven thousand Jewish people were smuggled into Sweden.

5. C. Close friends show they care during times of trouble.

6. H. People kept the Jewish people's apartments clean in their absence.

7. Students should write something about a dream of a better world where people live happily, trusting and caring for each other.

8. A. "Surely that gift—the gift of a world of human decency—is the one that all countries hunger for still."